U.S. ARMED FORCES

U.S. ARMY SPECIAL OPERATIONS FORCES

JEREMY ROBERTS

LERNER PUBLICATIONS COMPANY / MINNEAPOLIS

CHAPTER OPENER PHOTO CAPTIONS

Cover: Members of the U.S. Army Rangers dressed in camouflage suits look through sights attached to machine guns.

Ch. 1: U.S. Army troops fight on the front line during the advance on northern Baghdad in 2003 in the war in Iraq.

Ch. 2: U.S. Rangers participate in training exercises at the headquarters of the U.S. Army Special Operations Command at Fort Bragg, North Carolina.

Ch. 3: A soldier fast ropes (drops out of a helicopter using a rope) onto the deck of a ship.

Ch. 4: A U.S. Army Ranger team conducts a patrol through a swamp.

Lerner Publications Company
A division of Lerner Publishing Group
241 First Avenue North
Minneapolis, MN 55401 U.S.A.

Website address: www.lernerbooks.com

Library of Congress Cataloging-in-Publication Data

Roberts, Jeremy, 1956–
    U.S. Army Special Operations Forces / by Jeremy Roberts.
        p.   cm. — (U.S. Armed Forces)
    Includes bibliographical references and index.
    ISBN: 0–8225–1646–2 (lib. bdg. : alk. paper)
    1. United States Army Special Operations Command—Juvenile literature. I. Title:
United States Army Special Operations Forces. II. Title. III. Series: U.S. Armed Forces
(Series : Lerner Publications)
UA34.S64R63 2005
356'.16'0973—dc22   2004002963

Manufactured in the United States of America
1 2 3 4 5 6 – JR – 10 09 08 07 06 05

Contents

chapter ONE
HISTORY

DURING THE WAR IN IRAQ in 2003,
some U.S. Army soldiers were rushing supplies to the
battlefield. Their trucks took a wrong turn. Before they
knew it, they were in enemy territory and under fire.
Over the next several hours, a battle raged. Several
Americans were killed. Others surrendered and were
taken prisoner.

One of the prisoners was Private Jessica Lynch,
a 19-year-old woman from a small town in West
Virginia. Wounded, Private Lynch was taken to an

Iraqi hospital. She was held there under guard. She feared for her life and worried that she would be killed like some of her comrades.

About a week after her capture, some Iraqis told U.S. troops where Private Lynch was being held. Army special operations units sprang into action. On the night of March 31, Army Rangers and other special troops flew to the enemy town by helicopter. Wearing night vision goggles so they could see in the dark, the Rangers quickly took over the area around the hospital. Suddenly, soldiers burst into Lynch's room.

"Jessica Lynch, we're United States soldiers here, and we're here to protect you and take you home!" said one.

"I'm an American soldier, too," she replied. A few hours later, Lynch was safe and in a U.S. military hospital.

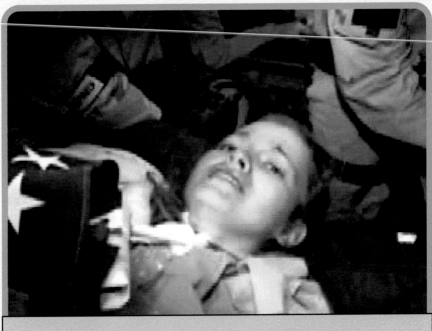

Jessica Lynch was rescued by U.S. special operators.

Many details of the mission remain secret, but news reports say that much of the work was done by members of the army's Special Operations Command, including Rangers. The Rangers and other members of the Special Operations Command are among the best fighters in the world.

SPECIAL SOLDIERS, SPECIAL MISSIONS

The military term *special operations* describes a mission that is out of the ordinary, or unlike conventional warfare. In conventional warfare, units with many soldiers attack across a wide area. They often use large numbers of tanks and aircraft. The attacking army tries to push back the enemy and take over its territory.

Special operations units attack in ways the enemy might not expect. Only a few soldiers—sometimes six or even less—will take part in an attack. Usually, the

Special operations are carried out by small groups of soldiers.

Most special operations are kept secret, even after they end. That's because military leaders don't want enemies to find out about their methods. In fact, nearly the only time Americans hear about special operations is when they fail. For each failure, however, there are many successes.

units do not try to capture territory. They might attempt a rescue behind enemy lines, as in the case of Private Lynch. They might blow up an important bridge the enemy needs. They might work with local people who are trying to overthrow their government. They might scout out enemy positions from a mountaintop, so that generals know how to best attack or defend against the enemy.

Some special missions don't involve fighting at all. For instance, sometimes special operations units perform humanitarian missions. They take food to starving people or take doctors and nurses to places where they're needed. The U.S. Army has many different units for such special missions. Their work is as old as fighting itself. In fact, armies were using special troops long before the United States became a nation.

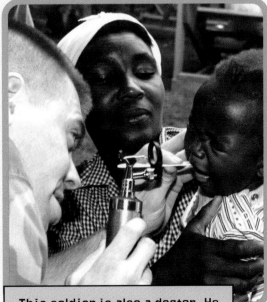

This soldier is also a doctor. He is giving medical care to a young Haitian boy.

EARLY SPECIAL TROOPS

Before Europeans arrived, Native Americans, or Indians, lived in North America. Indian warriors often used special tactics (ways of fighting). Small groups of warriors sometimes launched surprise raids against their enemies. A few Native Americans would travel great distances on foot or in canoes. They would emerge from the wilderness and strike the enemy without warning. Then they would slip away.

When Europeans began to settle in North America in the 1600s, they sometimes clashed with their Native American neighbors. Native warriors continued to use surprise tactics against the newcomers.

Both sides used special tactics during the French and Indian War.

European settlers in North America quickly adopted these tactics. During the French and Indian War (1754–1763), Major Robert Rogers divided his men into small groups. He called them rangers and taught them how to fight in the wilderness using special tactics.

During the American Revolution (1775–1783), the American colonies fought for their independence from Great Britain. While most of the war was fought by large units on big battlefields, at times small American forces struck behind British lines. These forces played an important role in the war. The most famous force was led by Francis Marion, who had learned his tactics fighting the Cherokee people. During their first battle against the British, Marion and his men attacked British troops who were trying to capture Charleston, South Carolina. After the British took over the city,

Robert Rogers *(pointing)* taught his rangers the fighting tactics of Native Americans.

Marion and 150 men hid in the nearby hills. They attacked small groups of British soldiers, striking quickly and then running away. This kind of fighting is sometimes called guerrilla warfare. Marion's fighters also captured British supplies such as food and weapons. Eventually, Marion's fighters helped force the British from the city.

Both sides used rangers during the American Civil War (1861–1865). The bloody conflict was fought between the Northern and Southern states. On the Southern side, Colonel John S. Mosby led bands of 50 or fewer men on raids deep inside enemy territory. They wrecked Northern supply houses and scouted for enemy forces. On the Northern side, Captain Samuel Means's Loudoun Rangers also attacked and confused the enemy. They even captured some of Mosby's men.

John S. Mosby *(left)* led a band of Southern guerrillas in the Civil War. Samuel Means's *(right)* troops fought for the North.

U.S. soldiers and British commandos fought together during World War II. Here commandos arrive ashore by boat.

RANGERS LEAD THE WAY!

World War II (1939–1945) took place in Europe, North Africa, Asia, and the Pacific Ocean. The United States joined the fighting in 1941. It fought alongside Great Britain, the Soviet Union, China, and other nations against Germany, Japan, and Italy. Looking for new ways to attack the Germans, the British formed special units called commandos. These forces snuck behind enemy lines to fight unconventionally. They blew up important enemy bases and destroyed railroads, for example. The British suggested that the Americans form commando units of their own.

The Americans agreed. They chose the name Rangers for their special troops. Their slogan was "Rangers Lead the Way." Their leader was William Orlando Darby. Soon, Rangers were fighting all over Europe. Some worked with British commandos on special raids. Others helped regular U.S. forces take over North Africa, Italy, France (which was then under German control), and finally Germany itself.

One Ranger specialty was amphibious assaults. These involved traveling from sea to fight on land. An amphibious assault can surprise the enemy, but it can be very dangerous. During D-Day, when the United States and its allies invaded German-controlled France, Rangers took on a difficult challenge. They landed beneath cliffs at a place called Pointe du Hoc. They climbed the cliffs using special rocket-propelled ropes and extension ladders. At every step, German machine-gun bullets and shells rained down on them. Many Rangers were killed or wounded.

Rangers also fought against the Japanese in Asia and on islands in the Pacific Ocean. In the

Modern amphibious vehicles land on a beach.

Merrill's Marauders march through a river that winds its way through the dense jungles of Burma.

Philippines, in January 1945, a Ranger unit struck behind enemy lines. During a bold raid, they freed 511 prisoners of war. These Americans were sick and starving. Some of them couldn't walk. To get the men back to safety 30 miles away, some Rangers carried other men on their backs.

One of the most famous special units of World War II was called Merrill's Marauders. They marched through mountains and jungles to fight the Japanese in the Asian nation of Burma, later called Myanmar. Though greatly outnumbered, Merrill's Marauders destroyed larger forces and captured an airport.

These new recruits became soldiers in the Korean War.

In 1950 the army trained a group of Rangers to parachute out of airplanes. Called Army Airborne Rangers, the men first fought in the Korean War (1950–1953). The unit consisted of 13 companies of about 112 men each. They were trained to fight at night, often parachuting into hostile territory. They also attacked behind enemy lines and scouted enemy positions.

NEW UNITS

Another special operations unit, called Special Forces, was created in 1952. This was during the Cold War (1945–1991). The Cold War was a time of great distrust between the United States and the Soviet Union. The two nations did not fight each other, but they often took opposite sides in wars involving other countries. U.S. and European leaders worried that the Soviet Union might invade the countries of Western Europe.

Like Rangers, Special Forces soldiers were trained for scouting missions and raids behind enemy lines. But they were also taught how to form local armies. That way, if the Soviet Union were to take over a foreign country, Special Forces troops could sneak into the nation disguised as civilians (people who aren't in the military). There, they could help local people form resistance armies to free themselves from Soviet control.

To do this kind of work, Special Forces soldiers needed special skills. For example, they had to speak foreign languages. They also had to be creative and clever, since they would sometimes work in disguise. Special Forces soldiers soon earned the nickname Green Berets because they normally wore green berets, a kind of hat.

AIRBORNE TROOPS

Soldiers who jump out of airplanes are called paratroopers or airborne units. Nearly all Rangers and Special Forces troops are trained to jump out of airplanes. The official names of some special operations units include the word *airborne*, such as Special Forces Group (Airborne). Not all paratroopers in the U.S. Army are Rangers or Special Forces soldiers, however.

Soldiers in Vietnam were taken into battle by helicopter.

The Vietnam War (1954–1975) took place in Southeast Asia. During part of the war, the United States helped South Vietnam in its fight against North Vietnam. Special Forces soldiers helped organize small local armies in South Vietnam. They also helped train South Vietnam's regular soldiers. Rangers also fought in the Vietnam War. They went on long-range patrols, searching for the enemy in Vietnam's thick jungle.

Starting in the 1970s, terrorists began attacking civilians around the world. Sometimes they hijacked (took over) airplanes. Sometimes they bombed airplanes or other targets. The terrorists used such tactics to call attention to their political causes. The United States needed a force to fight terrorists. So the army created a new unit called Delta Force, which was part of Special Forces.

Under the command of Colonel Charles A. Beckwith, Delta operators were trained for many jobs. One of the most important jobs was rescuing hostages. In 1980 Delta operators tried to rescue U.S. hostages being held in the Middle Eastern nation of Iran. After the unit had landed secretly in Iran, two of its helicopters had engine trouble. The mission was called off. As the Delta operators were getting ready to return, an airplane and a helicopter crashed. Several Delta operators were killed. The hostages were not freed until Iran released them many months later.

NEW CONFLICTS

Rangers led the way again in Panama in 1989. Panama was ruled by a military general named Manuel Noriega. He was a dishonest leader who allowed drug traffickers to operate in his country. The United States sent in troops

Delta Force operators lead attacks against terrorist bases.

Paratroopers were used in the attack against Manuel Noriega in Panama.

to overthrow Noriega. During the brief fight, Rangers jumped from airplanes and took over Panamanian airfields. Their surprise attack cleared the way for other U.S. troops to land. The forces helping Noriega gave up. Soon, Noriega surrendered too.

In 1990 forces from the Middle Eastern nation of Iraq invaded neighboring Kuwait. The United States joined forces with countries across the world to free Kuwait. The conflict was called the Persian Gulf War. Special operations units, including Special Forces and Rangers, performed several missions during the war. They hunted for missiles that Iraq had aimed at nearby countries. They also scouted on behalf of regular troops. Special Forces soldiers who could speak foreign languages worked as interpreters (people who turn words spoken in one language into another language). They helped commanders from the many foreign nations talk and work together.

After the war, Special Forces helped the Kurdish people, an ethnic group in northern Iraq. The Kurds opposed Iraq's government, and Iraqi forces had attacked them. As many as 600,000 Kurds fled into the mountains of northern Iraq without food or shelter. U.S. forces brought in 58,000 tons of food and other supplies, along with medicine. They protected the Kurds from the Iraqi army and helped them return home without being killed. Called Operation Provide Comfort, this project was one of the biggest humanitarian missions ever.

The Special Forces motto is *De oppresso liber.* That's Latin for "Free the oppressed," which means helping people who are being harmed by cruel rulers.

A helicopter takes Kurdish refugees to a refugee camp.

In 1992 Special Forces units went to the African country of Somalia to help people there. Many Somalis were starving. International aid organizations such as the United Nations Children's Fund (UNICEF) wanted to bring food and medicine to help. But fighting between local warlords (military leaders) made the situation too dangerous. In October 1993, a force of Rangers and Delta operators tried to capture one of the warlords. The warlord's army attacked the Americans. The special operators fought back, but they were greatly outnumbered. The Somalis killed 18 Americans. Despite this incident, the operation still helped many Somalis.

A Somali inspects the remains of a crashed Blackhawk helicopter. The pilot of the helicopter died in the crash.

THE WAR ON TERROR

On September 11, 2001, terrorists hijacked four U.S. airliners. They crashed two of the planes into the World Trade Center towers in New York City. They

The terrorist attack on September 11, 2001,
caused much damage to the Pentagon.

crashed another plane into the Pentagon, the U.S.
military headquarters near Washington, D.C. The
fourth plane crashed in a field in Pennsylvania. About
3,000 people were killed in the attacks.

The terrorists were members of a group called al-
Qaeda. Al-Qaeda was based in Afghanistan. The Taliban,
a group that controlled the Afghan government,
supported the terrorists. The United States sent troops
to Afghanistan to destroy al-Qaeda bases. Special
Forces units also worked with local leaders to fight
the Taliban. After the Taliban was defeated, Special
Forces troops remained in Afghanistan to keep
fighting al-Qaeda and to help rebuild the country.

Special operations soldiers helped capture Iraq's former leader, Saddam Hussein, in 2003.

A unit of Special Forces soldiers and Central Intelligence Agency (CIA) officers hunted for more terrorists and their leaders after the war.

The United States went to war in Iraq again in 2003. The United States wanted to overthrow Saddam Hussein, Iraq's leader. The full story of the war in Iraq has not yet been written. Most of the special operations there remain classified, or secret. Some missions may never be known. But special operations units most likely took a very active role in the war, including the December 2003 capture of Saddam Hussein himself.

chapter TWO

RECRUITMENT

THE U.S. ARMY Special Operations Command
is headquartered at Fort Bragg, North Carolina. It has
several different units. The most well-known groups are
the combat units, the Rangers and Special Forces. Delta
Force is part of Special Forces. A group called the 160th
Special Operations Aviation Regiment (SOAR) flies
helicopters for the combat units. A group called Civil
Affairs specializes in rebuilding places damaged by war
or natural disasters. A group called Psychological
Operations (PSYOP) uses written and spoken messages
to persuade enemies to surrender instead of fight.

This soldier in the Special Operations Support Command prepares Thanksgiving dinner for soldiers in Afghanistan.

Special Operations Support Command (SOSCOM) provides support services such as health care, communications, and equipment maintenance for the other special operations units. The John F. Kennedy Special Warfare Center and School is responsible for training special operations troops. In total, the U.S. Army Special Operations Command includes more than 20,000 soldiers.

JOINING THE ARMY

The first step in joining Special Operations Command is to join the U.S. Army itself. Anyone interested in joining the U.S. Army must first talk to a local army recruiter. Nearly all large cities and many towns have recruiting offices. Recruiters often visit high schools and youth groups to tell young people about the challenges and benefits of serving in the army. High school guidance counselors also help students learn about joining the army.

When new soldiers join the army, they take the
U.S. Army's oath of enlistment.

The army has two kinds of soldiers: enlisted
soldiers and officers. Officers are the leaders in the
army. They tell other soldiers what to do. Most
members of the army are enlisted soldiers.

The army includes three main groups. The first is
the regular army, sometimes called the active-duty
army. Its members are full-time soldiers. The second
group is the Army Reserve. Third is the National
Guard. Army Reserve and National Guard soldiers
serve in the army part-time. Most of them also hold jobs

These National Guard members were called into action for the war in Iraq.

outside the army or attend college. During an emergency, such as wartime, guard and reserve members can be called to active duty. (Members of the National Guard also help out in local and state emergencies.)

To join the U.S. Army, a young man or woman must be between the ages of 17 and 35. He or she must be a U.S. citizen or a citizen of a foreign country living legally in the United States. He or she must be in good health and good physical shape. Recruits, or new soldiers, must agree to serve for eight years, with at least two years on active duty. The soldier can serve the remaining years in the Army Reserve.

Recruits take a series of tests called the Armed Services Vocational Aptitude Battery (ASVAB). The tests measure a recruit's language, math, mechanical, and scientific knowledge. The test results tell the army what skills the recruit has and what army job would be a good fit for the recruit.

Next, recruits go through training programs. They start with nine weeks of basic training. At this training, recruits exercise and learn basic fighting skills, such as how to fire guns. They also learn to follow orders. After basic training, soldiers train for specific army jobs. The army has more than 200 jobs, everything from construction to

cooking to computer repair. The army tries to give soldiers jobs they want. Some soldiers choose a combat job, such as being in the infantry as a foot soldier, being a combat engineer, or being a member of a tank crew. Most soldiers who want to join special operations start out in combat jobs.

These soldiers had to go through basic training and serve in the army before joining Special Forces.

UNIFORMS

ALL SOLDIERS IN THE ARMY MUST WEAR UNIFORMS.
You can tell a soldier's name, rank, and job just by
looking at his or her uniform. The army issues different
uniforms for different occasions, jobs, and roles. On
some missions, Special Forces soldiers wear clothes that
do not identify them as soldiers at all. They might dress
like the civilians around them. Or they might
wear all black, to blend in with the night.

DRESS UNIFORM

For ceremonies and special occasions,
enlisted soldiers wear dark green
trousers, dark green jackets, light
green shirts, and black ties. Officers
wear a similar uniform. Their pants
have black stripes on the sides.

Soldiers also wear woolen berets
with their dress uniforms. The berets
are marked with the insignia (symbol)
of the soldier's unit. Special Forces
soldiers wear green berets, airborne
troops wear maroon berets, and Rangers
wear tan berets. Soldiers also wear
ribbons and medals pinned to their dress
uniforms. These decorations symbolize
a soldier's achievements.

When working in an office, soldiers wear a less formal dress uniform. It has the same green shirt and pants, but it is usually worn without a jacket and tie.

Battle Dress Uniform

During combat or training, soldiers usually wear battle dress uniforms (BDUs). The BDU includes pants and a shirt, with a jacket for extra warmth. The uniform comes in different styles and colors, depending on the weather and combat area. For example, soldiers fighting in a desert might wear a BDU with a "chocolate chip" camouflage pattern. This tan and brown pattern blends in well with the desert background, making the soldier hard to see. Soldiers in combat usually wear bulletproof vests and helmets. They might also wear airtight suits that offer protection from chemical or biological weapons.

JOINING SPECIAL OPERATIONS

Each special operations unit has its own rules about joining. The requirements and tests are tough. Soldiers must be in top condition, both physically and mentally, to join these units. Many soldiers want to join special operations, but not everyone who applies gets accepted.

WOMEN IN DELTA FORCE?

Officially, no women are allowed in combat positions in Special Operations Command. However, Delta Force is rumored to include a special group of female soldiers. If this is true, information about this group, like all Delta units and operations, is secret. Few people know for sure if the female Delta operators really exist.

Combat jobs are off-limits to women in the army. So only men can join Rangers, Special Forces, and SOAR as combat soldiers. Women can hold support positions in these units, however. For instance, they can work behind the scenes in office jobs.

Most soldiers apply to become Rangers after they are already in the army. They must have their commanding officers' approval to apply. They must be U.S. citizens and in excellent physical shape. They

Women are not allowed to serve in combat positions in the army, but they do important jobs that support combat soldiers.

must also have experience in another army combat job. Some recruits apply to become Rangers when they first join the army.

To join Special Forces or Delta Force, soldiers must usually hold the rank of sergeant or above. They must be at least 22 years old and must be in good physical condition. Most important, soldiers must show themselves to be smart, inventive, and creative. They must pass many physical tests that measure their skills in difficult circumstances.

The 160th SOAR includes helicopter pilots, crew members who assist pilots in flight, and others. Soldiers who want to join SOAR as pilots must already be army pilots. They must have 1,000 hours of experience flying army helicopters, including 100 hours flying at night. They must be physically fit and pass a review by other pilots and officers.

The 160th SOAR operates helicopters, such as the Black Hawk above, for the Army Special Forces.

For crew members and mechanics who want to join SOAR, the requirements differ from job to job.

Joining PSYOP or Civil Affairs is much like joining any other unit in the army. Both men and women can serve in these units. Each job has different requirements. For example, a soldier who wants to run radio equipment for PSYOP might need previous experience running radio equipment. He or she might also need a recommendation from a commanding officer. Many people who work in PSYOP or Civil Affairs are reservists. They spend most of the year working in nonmilitary jobs and work for the army part-time.

OTHER SPECIAL UNITS

Other branches of the U.S. military, such as the navy and the air force, also have special operations units. For instance, the navy's special operations troops are called SEALs, which stands for *sea, air,* and *land.*

chapter THREE

TRAINING

SOLDIERS CHOSEN to work in special operations must go through advanced training. Ranger candidates (students) begin their training at Fort Benning in Georgia. For several weeks, they take introductory classes on subjects such as fighting terrorism and the history of the Rangers. They also learn basic Ranger skills, such as dropping out of helicopters using ropes. To go forward in the program, Ranger candidates must pass physical tests, such as hiking, running, and chin-up tests.

Ranger candidates who pass the first program then take a 61-day course. During this course, Ranger candidates crawl through muddy trenches laced with barbed wire. They parachute from helicopters and climb down cliffs at night. Finally, for nine days, they live in swamps and woods. They make their way through "enemy" territory to fight a mock battle on an island near Fort Benning. It may be just a test, but it's still dangerous. Several men have died during the training.

Ranger classes generally start with about 220 soldiers. But usually only about 125 pass the course. Some candidates drop out, while others fail their tests. Soldiers who don't make it through Ranger training are given different assignments in the army. Some return to their old units.

SPECIAL FORCES TRAINING

Special Forces training is tough too. It begins with a 21-day evaluation course at Fort Bragg, North Carolina. There, experienced Special Forces soldiers

WHAT'S IN A NAME?

The name Ranger is used to label soldiers in the 75th Ranger Regiment, the official Ranger unit. But the name also applies to any soldier who has gone through Ranger training. This training is open to members of all branches of the U.S. military who can meet certain requirements. For instance, a U.S. Marine can be a Ranger, and several are.

At the end of the Ranger training course, the soldiers go back to their regular units and share their skills with other members. They wear a black-and-gold tab on their uniforms, like all other Rangers, but they are not members of the 75th Ranger Regiment.

This lieutenant takes a physical fitness test as part of the training to become a Ranger military intelligence officer.

evaluate the trainees. The trainees take mental health and physical fitness tests. They are pushed to their physical limits to see how much stress they can take.

Those who pass the evaluation begin official Special Forces training. This training is also very difficult. Out of every 100 soldiers who start the program, only about 45 finish. In the first 40 days of training, soldiers practice basic skills, such as shooting and handling different kinds of weapons. For the next 65 days, they learn to perform other jobs, such as operating antitank missiles and foreign machine guns or using radios. For the final 38 days, trainees come together to use their skills as a team. They practice tactics that might be used in wartime behind enemy lines.

TOOLS OF THE TRADE

SPECIAL OPERATORS use many different kinds of weapons and tools. Each piece of equipment does an important job.

GUNS

Like other soldiers in the army, special operators use the M16 assault rifle. They also use the M4A1 *(right)*, a smaller, lighter version of the M16. Because the M4A1 is smaller, it is easier to handle and carry, especially for a soldier parachuting behind enemy lines.

The MP5 is a lightweight submachine gun. It is small, but it packs a big punch. The M249 SAW (squad automatic weapon) is a heavier machine gun. It can fire many bullets at one time.

Snipers use the M24 rifle. It is fitted with a telescope for long-range shooting. Snipers also use the Barrett M82A1A rifle. It fires big bullets that can damage trucks and other large vehicles.

NIGHT OPTICAL DEVICES

For fighting at night, special operators use night optical devices (NODs). NODs are goggles that allow fighters to see in the dark. Some NODs work by magnifying available light. Others detect infrared light (energy waves put off by heat).

COMMUNICATIONS EQUIPMENT

The AN/PSC5 is a heavy and powerful radio. It can communicate through satellites (spacecraft orbiting above the earth). A soldier can use this radio to talk to people on the other side of the battlefield or the other side of the country.

AIRPLANES

Special operations units often parachute from C-130 Hercules airplanes *(above)* or C-17s, large jet-powered cargo planes. Some C-130 Hercules planes can fly very low to the ground, where they can avoid enemy radar equipment.

Special operations forces often use these same aircraft to drop supplies to troops and people in need.

HELICOPTERS

The basic army helicopter is the Blackhawk *(left)*. A larger helicopter, the Chinook, is often used for long-range missions. Nicknamed the Little Bird, the AH6 is a small helicopter, only about 6 feet wide and 22 feet long from nose to tail. Its small size helps make it quick and easy to maneuver.

As part of a training exercise, U.S. Army Rangers prepare to search out enemy troops in a dense forest.

For their final exam, trainees infiltrate, or sneak into, dense woods. They meet up with pretend resistance forces. The students help organize the resistance forces and fight their enemy. The exercise isn't real, but it's very similar to actual Special Forces missions.

Students who pass the final exam take more classes and special training. They might learn new foreign languages or polish the language skills they already have. They might learn to blow up bridges or mend broken arms. They might take advanced scuba diving training. They might also learn how to disguise themselves as residents of foreign countries, so they will fit in on missions.

THE JOHN F. KENNEDY SPECIAL WARFARE CENTER AND SCHOOL

Based in Fort Bragg, North Carolina, the John F. Kennedy Special Warfare Center and School is responsible for training special operations soldiers. The unit is called the army's "special operations university."

SOAR TRAINING

Soldiers who are chosen to join SOAR attend a training program called Green Platoon. This course takes place at Fort Campbell, Kentucky. It lasts five weeks for crew members and up to eight months for pilots. Students in Green Platoon review basic aviation skills. They practice flying and working at night. They also take classes in survival skills, medical care, and other subjects.

In the cockpit of a U.S. Army Chinook helicopter, the copilot *(right)* studies a map, while the pilot *(left)* flies the helicopter.

PSYOP AND CIVIL AFFAIRS TRAINING

Most soldiers in Psychological Operations and Civil
Affairs do not go through intense physical and combat
training. Most of them are members of National Guard
or Army Reserve units.

Most already have a great deal of experience in the
army. But these soldiers must still take special classes
to learn the skills necessary for their jobs. A Civil
Affairs soldier, for example, might learn how to help
people after a natural disaster, such as a hurricane.
The soldier might learn how to administer first aid and

Civil Affairs soldiers oversee the construction
of new schools in Afghanistan.

set up emergency shelters.

One Civil Affairs unit is specially trained in airborne operations. Its members know how to parachute into disaster areas or war zones to assist civilians.

Besides taking army courses, some Civil Affairs and PSYOP soldiers attend civilian colleges. There they study subjects that will help them with their army work. Examples for Civil Affairs soldiers include engineering, government, and business.

PSYOP soldiers might take classes in communications, studying how to create effective TV and radio messages. They might take classes in psychology, so they can better understand how people think and behave. They might study the language and culture of a foreign nation, to enable them to communicate better with the citizens there.

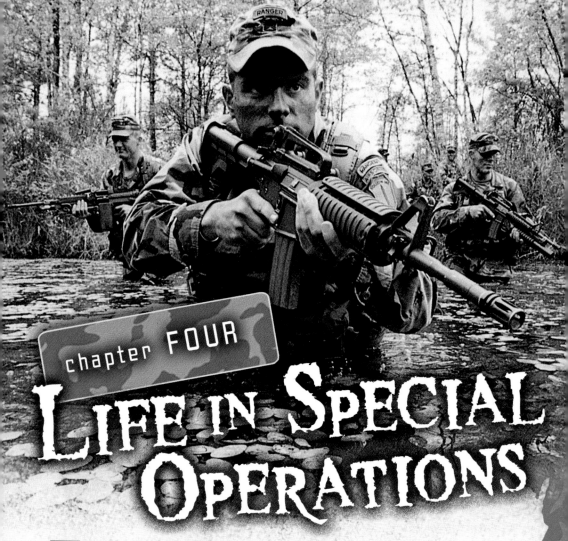

chapter FOUR

LIFE IN SPECIAL OPERATIONS

THERE IS NO "TYPICAL DAY"

for special operations soldiers. Depending on their unit and mission, the soldiers might have to leave for a foreign country at a moment's notice. They might find themselves behind enemy lines or fighting enemy troops. Much of the time, Rangers and Special Forces soldiers spend their days training and improving their fighting skills.

Many soldiers in PSYOP and Civil Affairs are reservists. They spend much of the year working at civilian jobs, until an emergency calls them to duty. Soldiers who work for SOSCOM or the John F. Kennedy Special Warfare Center and School usually work behind the scenes, doing office work, planning and organizing, and teaching other special operations soldiers.

LIFE IN RANGERS

Army Rangers are "war fighters." Their main job is to fight in combat. In the army's terms, they are "light infantry." *Light* means that Rangers do not travel with heavy equipment such as tanks and artillery (big guns that shoot large shells). Therefore, they can respond quickly to a combat situation. They are more flexible than other units. *Infantry* refers to soldiers who fight on foot.

The 75th Ranger Regiment is the name of the overall Ranger organization. The regiment includes three battalions. A headquarters unit commands and coordinates the work of the three battalions. Each battalion is made up of three rifle companies, each with its own headquarters unit. Each rifle company has about 100 men, although

Rangers advance on foot carrying M-16 machine guns.

units can be a little larger or smaller. Each company can be divided into smaller units for special missions.

Each Ranger battalion must be ready to go to war with only 18 hours notice. To prepare for this job, Rangers spend much of the year practicing their fighting skills. They practice jumping out of airplanes and landing on beaches. They train with weapons such as mortars and machine guns. Rangers often take part in large mock battles with other army groups.

FOOTBALL STAR TO WAR HERO

In 2002 Pat Tillman walked away from his career as a defensive back in the National Football League to join the 75th Ranger Regiment. Tillman fought in Iraq in 2003 and was killed in action in Afghanistan in 2004. Friends, family, and teammates remember him for his bravery and patriotism.

LIFE IN SPECIAL FORCES

Special Forces soldiers perform a number of different jobs and missions. These missions include scouting enemy positions, raiding enemy railroads and bridges, and making rescues behind enemy lines. Sometimes Special Forces units train foreign troops or other U.S. troops in new war-fighting skills. Because of their language skills, Special Forces soldiers also work with government officials as interpreters. They might work undercover, or secretly, carrying out missions for the CIA or another government agency.

The basic Special Forces combat unit is called an A team. Ordinarily, each team has 12 enlisted men. But the team can be broken into different parts, most often two six-member teams.

LIFE IN SOAR

The army's 160th SOAR flies helicopters for other special operations units. For instance, SOAR pilots and crew members take Rangers and Special Forces soldiers behind enemy lines and on other combat missions. At the target, the helicopter might land and let out the troops. Or it might hover above the ground, while the soldiers use special ropes to rappel, or slide down, to the ground.

SOAR pilots and crew members fly most of their missions at night. They call themselves the Night Stalkers. Special night vision goggles that use infrared light (similar to heat waves) help them see in the dark.

A Blackhawk helicopter drops off a soldier in a clearing in the woods.

A helicopter pilot adjusts his night vision goggles before a night mission.

Mechanics spend many hours keeping this Chinook helicopter and other helicopters used for special operations in working order.

SOAR pilots fly very low to avoid enemy radar. (Radar is a device that uses radio waves to locate objects far away.) They also use special communication devices to "talk" to satellites that tell them where they are. The pilots fly fast, making it hard for enemies to shoot them down. Members' jobs are very dangerous. When they are not on missions, they must work intensely to perfect their skills.

SOAR also includes mechanics and other experts who keep helicopters working. For every hour a helicopter is in the air, mechanics spend many more hours checking equipment, repairing engines, replacing worn parts, and testing new gear.

LIFE IN PSYOP

During the wars in Iraq in 1991 and 2003, U.S. troops took thousands of prisoners. The prisoners often surrendered to the Americans without a fight. Why? Because PSYOP soldiers had been working for months to convince them to surrender. The soldiers used a tactic called psychological warfare. This kind of warfare involves fighting with words and ideas instead of with guns and other weapons.

PSYOP soldiers used several methods in Iraq. They created fliers using pictures and simple words in Arabic (the main language of Iraq). The fliers told Iraqi troops that the United States and its allies would not harm them if they surrendered. The fliers also told the Iraqis how to surrender by setting down or leaving their weapons. PSYOP soldiers created radio programs with the same information. They dropped the fliers from airplanes and broadcast the radio messages before the

This soldier is dropping pamphlets from a helicopter to the Iraqi soldiers and civilians as part of U.S. operations in 2003.

A PSYOP soldier gives radios to the leader of a village in Afghanistan. The villagers will be able to listen to radio messages created by PSYOP members.

fighting began. Some PSYOP units worked with combat troops on the front lines. They used loudspeakers to tell enemy soldiers how to surrender safely.

PSYOP soldiers also worked in other Middle Eastern countries during the war. They wanted people in the Middle East to understand why the United States was fighting in Iraq. They built support for the United States with radio and television messages explaining U.S. views. PSYOP soldiers sometimes create these kinds of messages in peacetime as well. The messages help improve relations between the United States and foreign countries. PSYOP soldiers also learn about customs used in foreign countries and teach other soldiers how to get along well with foreigners.

A SPECIAL MISSION

The helicopter sped across the desert just a few feet off the ground. The night was cold. The open door let the air whip around the small cabin, where the three Special Forces soldiers were huddled, waiting to be dropped off. It was January 1991, during the Persian Gulf War. The three men had been chosen for a classic Special Forces mission— special reconnaissance, or scouting. The helicopter was about to leave them deep inside Iraq. They would hide there and watch a nearby road. If enemy troops drove along it, they would use a radio to warn regular troops many miles south.

It was a dangerous mission, deep in the heart of enemy territory. But the men had spent weeks practicing. They were ready for anything.

The helicopter swooped down. The men jumped to the ground, hauling their gear. They worked quickly, digging into the ground to make a "hide"—a narrow trench that could be camouflaged, or disguised, to blend in with the terrain.

Night became morning. The men took turns sleeping.

Suddenly, they heard an odd sound nearby, unlike anything they had trained for. It wasn't the noise of tanks or an army advancing. It sounded like children playing.

Children playing? How could that be?

It was children playing. The intelligence the team had received was not accurate. They had been put in an area where civilians lived.

The children and their parents soon discovered the soldiers. But rather than attack civilians, the men calmly called for another helicopter to pick them up. In a way, the mission was a failure. But the story shows how the unexpected can happen in wartime. And it shows Special Forces soldiers at their best—not using force against civilians but using patience and careful judgment instead.

INSIGNIA

EVERYONE IN THE ARMY HAS A RANK, or position of authority. Soldiers with higher ranks command those with lower ranks. Soldiers must always follow orders given by those who outrank them.

The lowest rank in the army is private E-1. Recruits start at that rank after enlistment. If privates do what they are told and do their jobs well, they will be promoted to a higher rank. They will be given more pay and more responsibilities. Below are some army insignias, starting with the lowest rank and moving up to the highest.

ENLISTED PERSONNEL

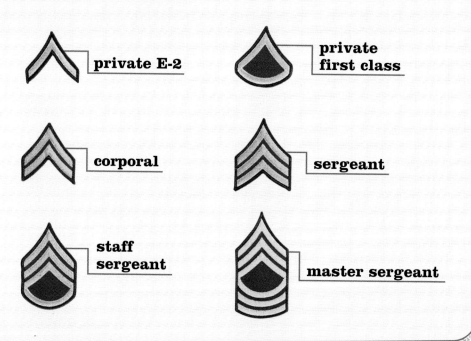

private E-2

private first class

corporal

sergeant

staff sergeant

master sergeant

OFFICERS

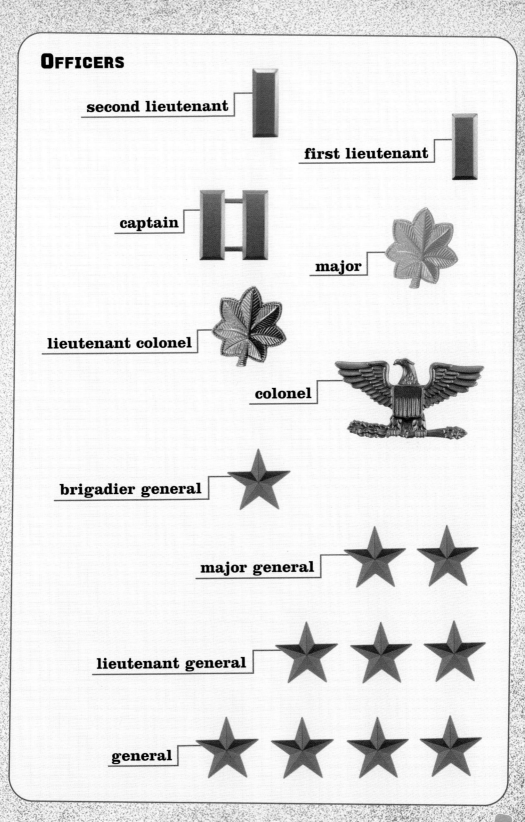

second lieutenant

first lieutenant

captain

major

lieutenant colonel

colonel

brigadier general

major general

lieutenant general

general

The army has about 1,200 full-time PSYOP soldiers. Another 3,600 PSYOP soldiers are members of the Army Reserve. The full-time soldiers are members of the Fourth Psychological Operations Group (Airborne). Like other airborne soldiers, they are trained to parachute out of airplanes.

LIFE IN CIVIL AFFAIRS

How do you govern a city after a war or a natural disaster? How do you get the electricity running? How do you find guards for the jail? Civil Affairs soldiers are trained to answer these questions and solve these problems.

Following the Persian Gulf War in 1991, Civil Affairs soldiers flew to northern Iraq. They arranged to drop food from airplanes to help starving Kurds. They also met with local leaders. They helped Kurds who had fled

Civil Affairs soldiers gather information in Samawa, Iraq, to help improve the Iraqi water system.

CHANGING TACTICS

In the twentieth century, psychological operations sometimes included lies and trickery. During World War II, for instance, the Japanese government broadcast its infamous "Tokyo Rose" radio programs. The programs featured popular U.S. music of the time and female announcers who spoke English. But the announcers (whom the Americans nicknamed Tokyo Rose) told lies meant to discourage U.S. soldiers fighting in Asia. For instance, they told about U.S. troops running away from combat.

Modern PSYOP soldiers know they can do their job best by telling the truth instead of lying. In fact, most PSYOP soldiers say that lies are their worst enemies, since lies lead to mistrust. Instead of lies, modern PSYOP uses advertising techniques, such as colorful TV messages, to tell the truth about U.S. positions or beliefs.

their homes set up temporary camps and govern themselves.

Civil Affairs troops also worked in Haiti, an island nation in the Caribbean Sea, in 1994. They helped reorganize the Haitian military and police force after the country's president had fled. They also helped restore the country's judicial (court) system and helped plan new elections.

Army Civil Affairs troops went to Iraq after the United States ousted Saddam Hussein in 2003. After the major fighting ended, they helped rebuild power stations, reopen hospitals, and restore government systems.

The army has about 10,000 Civil Affairs soldiers. Most of them are in the National Guard. When not serving in the military, many of these soldiers work as judges, police officers, or government officials in their home communities.

THE FUTURE

Special Forces soldiers stand by during a ceremony presenting a new, improved helicopter.

What will special operations involve in the future? Certainly, Rangers and Special Forces will be involved in future wars. Their ability to fight in unconventional and unexpected ways will give them an edge in future combat situations. Civil Affairs soldiers will continue to work in such places as the Middle East and Africa, helping foreign citizens.

Special operators will probably use new equipment on missions. For instance, remote-controlled spy planes and satellites might send up-to-the-second pictures of the enemy directly to special operators on the battlefield. Tiny remote-controlled aircraft and vehicles may also help special operators on the battlefield.

It is hard to predict the future. But one thing is certain. Whenever the United States needs talented and dedicated troops to fight its most important missions, the U.S. Army Special Operations Command will be ready to take on the job.

STRUCTURE

ALL U.S. ARMY SPECIAL OPERATIONS UNITS, including the Rangers, Special Forces, 160th SOAR, Civil Affairs, PSYOP, and SOSCOM report to the U.S. Army Special Operations Command. The command is part of the Department of the Army, headed by the secretary of the army. This officer reports to the secretary of defense, who reports to the president of the United States.

PRESIDENT OF THE UNITED STATES

SECRETARY OF DEFENSE

U.S. ARMY SPECIAL OPERATIONS COMMAND

160TH SOAR

PSYOP

RANGERS

SOSCOM

SPECIAL FORCES

CIVIL AFFAIRS

TIMELINE

1756 During the French and Indian War, British units under Major Robert Rogers use ranger tactics.

1775-1783 The American Revolution is fought. Colonel Daniel Morgan's ranger unit helps bring about an American victory at Saratoga, New York, a turning point in the war. Francis Marion, called the Swamp Fox, leads another ranger unit during the war.

1861-1865 Both sides used rangers during the American Civil War. The most famous ranger unit is a Confederate force headed by John S. Mosby.

1942 During World War II, the U.S. Army begins training commando forces called Rangers.

1952 The U.S. Army creates the Special Forces. Its soldiers are trained to help form local resistance movements, gather information, and perform other missions for the regular army.

1959 Special Forces units arrive in Vietnam to help the South Vietnamese in their fight against the North Vietnamese.

1977 The U.S. Army creates Delta Force, designed to fight terrorists.

1989 U.S. troops invade Panama to overthrow its leader. Special Forces and Ranger units take part in the operation.

1991 Special operations units conduct missions inside enemy territory during the Persian Gulf War. PSYOP units help convince many Iraqis to surrender without a fight.

2001-2002 Special operations units strike back against al-Qaeda terrorists in Afghanistan.

2003 Army special operations forces capture Saddam Hussein, the former dictator of Iraq.

GLOSSARY

amphibious: operating on both water and land. The term describes military operations in which soldiers land on a beach from ships.

camouflage: patterned clothing or other material that allows soldiers to blend in with their surroundings

civilian: a person not involved in military service

conventional warfare: normal war operations, usually involving large units attacking over wide areas

guerrillas: small groups of fighters who operate independently. They use nontraditional military practices, trying to surprise their enemy and strike where they are not expected.

humanitarian mission: an effort to help people, such as the delivery of food to groups who are starving

infantry: a soldier who faces the enemy on foot with handheld weapons. The infantry is the largest fighting unit in the army.

infiltrate: to secretly enter an area, such as enemy territory

intelligence: information about the enemy

interpreter: a person who turns words from one language into another

psychological warfare: the use of information to convince the enemy not to fight or to wear down the enemy's will to fight

radar: a system that uses radio waves to detect objects such as planes and ships

reconnaissance: a military scouting expedition, used to gain information about the enemy

resistance: fighters in a conquered or invaded nation who strike back at the invading forces

satellite: a spacecraft that orbits the earth, often equipped with cameras or communications equipment

terrorism: the use of violence, such as bombing, to terrify civilians

war fighter: a soldier who handles weapons in combat

FAMOUS PEOPLE

Charles A. Beckwith (1929–1994) Beckwith, of Plains, Georgia, was a U.S. Special Forces officer who created Delta Force in the 1970s. He modeled the unit on British antiterrorist units. Beckwith is probably best known for a failed operation called Operation Eagle Claw. The operation was designed to rescue U.S. civilians being held hostage in Iran in 1980. However, because of equipment problems, Beckwith had to call off the operation during its early stages in the Iranian desert. An aircraft accident then claimed the lives of eight of his men.

William Orlando Darby (1911–1945) Arkansas native William Darby grew up in Fort Smith and attended the U.S. Military Academy at West Point, New York. He graduated in 1933. During World War II, the army had Darby form units similar to the British commandos. He called the units Rangers. Darby died during World War II in April 1945, when he was killed by an artillery shell.

Robert L. Howard (born 1939) Howard, a native of Opelika, Alabama, served in the U.S. Army for 36 years. He became one of the most honored soldiers in history. A member of Special Forces during the Vietnam War, he won a Congressional Medal of Honor for helping rescue an army unit behind enemy lines in Laos.

Robert D. Law (1944–1969) Law, born in Fort Worth, Texas, was the first member of a Ranger unit to win a Congressional Medal of Honor for service in Vietnam. In February 1969, he was on patrol in Vietnam when his unit came under fire. A grenade landed among the U.S. troops. Although he could have jumped for cover and saved himself, Law leaped on the grenade and saved the lives of his fellow soldiers. He died in the explosion.

Colin Powell (born 1937) Secretary of State Colin Powell was born in New York City. He entered Ranger school right after completing college in 1958. He went on to take airborne training and served in combat during the Vietnam War. He eventually rose to the army's highest rank, four-star general. During the Persian Gulf War, he served as chairman of the Joint Chiefs of Staff, the highest military adviser to the president. He became secretary of state in 2001.

Robert Rogers (1731–1795) Born in colonial New England in present-day Londonderry, New Hampshire, Rogers led a force called Rogers's Rangers during the French and Indian War. He fought on behalf of the British during that war. During the Revolutionary War, Rogers also fought on the side of the British, this time against the Americans. He led a unit called the Loyalist Queen's Rangers in that war.

Patrick Tillman (1976–2004) Born in San Jose, California, Tillman was a star defensive back for the Arizona Cardinals of the National Football League. After the September 11, 2001, attacks on the United States, Tillman gave up a multimillion-dollar football contract to join the U.S. Army Rangers. He fought in Iraq during the 2003 invasion, then was sent to Afghanistan, where he was killed in action in April 2004. Tillman was killed trying to save the lives of other soldiers. After his death, the army awarded Tillman a Silver Star, a special honor for bravery. He was also promoted to corporal because of his bravery and leadership skills.

BIBLIOGRAPHY

Alexander, David. *Tomorrow's Soldier.* New York: Avon Books, 1999.

Clancy, Tom, Carl Stiner, and Tony Koltz. *Shadow Warriors.* New York: G. P. Putnam's Sons, 2002.

Haney, Eric L. *Inside Delta Force.* New York: Delacorte Press, 2002.

Marquis, Susan L. *Unconventional Warfare.* Washington, DC: The Brookings Institution, 1977.

Means, Howard. *Colin Powell.* New York: Donald I. Fine, 1992.

Powell, Colin, and Joseph E. Persico. *Colin Powell.* New York: Random House, 1995.

Simons, Anna. *The Company They Keep: Life inside the U.S. Special Forces.* Boston: Free Press, 1997.

Southworth, Samuel A., and Stephen Tanner. *U.S. Special Forces.* Cambridge, MA: DaCapo Press, 2002.

Walker, Greg. *At the Hurricane's Eye.* New York: Ivy Books, 1994.

Waller, Douglas C. *The Commandos.* New York: Simon & Schuster, 1994.

FURTHER READING

Benson, Michael. *The U.S. Army.* Minneapolis: Lerner Publications Company, 2005.

Boher, David. *America's Special Forces.* Osceola, WI: MBI Publishing Company, 1998.

Burgan, Michael. *U.S. Army Special Forces: Airborne Rangers.* Bloomington, MN: Capstone Books, 2000.

Burnett, Betty. *Delta Force: Counterterrorism Unit of the U.S. Army.* New York: Rosen Central, 2003.

Cornish, Geoff. *Battlefield Support.* Minneapolis: Lerner Publications Company, 2003.

Dartford, Mark. *Helicopters.* Minneapolis: Lerner Publications Company, 2003.

McNab, Chris. *Survive in the Mountains with the U.S. Rangers and Army Mountain Division.* Broomall, PA: Mason Crest Publishers, 2003.

Visual Dictionary of Special Military Forces. London: Dorling Kindersley, 1993.

WEBSITES

Goarmy.com
<http://www.goarmy.com>
The army's recruiting site, this website provides basic
information about becoming a soldier. For soldiers who want
to join, this is a good starting place.

The United States Army Home Page
<http://www.army.mil>
This is the army's official website. It offers pages on army
history as well as current events.

U.S. Army John F. Kennedy Special Warfare Museum
<http://www.soc.mil/swcs/museum/museum.shtml>
The museum is dedicated to preserving and exhibiting
material related to the history of army special operations.
This website includes information on museum exhibits and
programs.

U.S. Army Ranger Association (USARA)
<http://www.ranger.org>
The U.S. Army Ranger Association's site contains Ranger
history and links for more information.

USASOC Home (U.S. Army Special Operations Command)
<http://www.soc.mil/hqs/hqs_home.htm>
The U.S. Army Special Operations Command website provides
a variety of news and information about the Rangers, SOAR,
Special Forces, and other special army units.

INDEX

PHOTO ACKNOWLEDGMENTS

The images in this book are used with the permission of:
© David Leeson/*Dallas Morning News*/CORBIS, p. 4; © Defense
Visual Information Center, pp. 5, 6, 19, 25, 27, 29, 30, 38, 39,
45 (right), 47; © U.S. Army Special Operations Command, pp. 7,
12, 15, 18, 22, 24, 31, 33, 35, 37 (bottom) 40, 42, 46, 48, 52, 54;
© Gary Zaboly, pp. 8, 9; Library of Congress, pp. 10 (left) [LC-
DIG-cwpbh-03240]; 11 [LC-USE6-D-008299], 16 [LC-USZ62-
122601]; © The Thomas Balch Library, p.10 (right); © Merrill's
Marauders Association, p. 13; courtesy of Harry Lerner, p.14;
© Mark H. Milstein/Northfoto/ZUMA Press, p.17; © Paul
Watson/Toronto Star/ZUMA Press, p. 20; © Tech. Sgt. Cedric H.
Rudisill/United States Department of Defense, p. 21; © Gary
Kieffer/ZUMA Press, p.23; © Jack Kurtz/ZUMA Press, p. 26;
© Wally McNamee/CORBIS, p. 28; © Global Specops, pp. 43, 45
(left); © Jim Sugar/CORBIS, p. 36; © George Hall/CORBIS, p. 37
(top); © Photography Plus C/O Stealth Media Solutions/
Reuters/CORBIS, p. 44; © Todd Strand/Independent Picture
Service, pp. 50 (all), 51 (all).

Cover image: © CORBIS